Copyright © 2013 by Tyler Hershberger

All rights reserved.

No part of this book may be used or reproduced
in any manner whatsoever without written permission of the author.

Printed in the United States of America
ISBN 978-1-484866191

Easy Read Publishers
4000 E. Bristol Street, Suite 3,
Elkhart, IN 46514

Table of Contents

Dedication 4
Introduction 5

Chapter 1 13
    That First 4 Seconds

Chapter 2 15
    Cut the Drama — Just Dance

Chapter 3 17
    Dance like No One's Looking

Chapter 4 19
    A $140,000 Sale in 15 Minutes

Chapter 5 21
    The Most Important Word in Selling Has Only Three Letters

Chapter 6 23
    How I Found Hidden Objections

Chapter 7 24
    The Art of the Dance Is Magic in Selling

Chapter 8 26
    Automate to Organize

Chapter 9 27
    Dancing Is All about Confidence

Chapter 10 29
    How to Look Your Best: the Sale

before the Sale

Chapter 11 31
How I Learned to Remember Names and Faces

Chapter 12 33
How I Find New Customers and Keep Old Ones

Chapter 13 35
"Two Left Feet"? No Problem!

Chapter 14 37
Enthusiasm-Boosters

Chapter 15 38
An Amazing Closing Technique I Learned from a 35-year-old Dance Veteran

Chapter 16 39
Don't Be Afraid to Fail

Chapter 17 41
Everyone's Got Rhythm

Chapter 22 43
If all else fails, remember:

DEDICATION

To Sally, my first instructor who taught me that I did have rhythm, and whose enthusiasm for ballroom dance was contagious. To Craig who gave me a chance just out of college to learn about sales on the ballroom floor and practice my skills for 4 years. To my wife, Sarah, who is the love of my life and who I will dance with forever. To my parents, Eldon and Nina, who loved me enough to pay for those expensive ballroom dance lessons and came to every one of my competitions. To my sister, Anya, who loved ballroom dancing as much as I did and was often my dance partner. And finally, to my German brother, Pascal. If it weren't for him I would never have learned to dance and this book would never have been written.

INTRODUCTION

About Me

Hi! My name is Tyler Hershberger. In these next few chapters, I'm going to share some secrets that I learned through an unusual occupation: ballroom dancing. I didn't go to school for sales or marketing, but what I did have was a passion for ballroom dancing. In order to tell you this part of my story, I will need to go back to 2002, when I first started ballroom dancing.

An Unexpected Beginning

When I was a junior in high school, my parents decided to host an exchange student. At first, we were going to host someone from Venezuela, but some unforeseen difficulties made it impossible for him to come. There was, however, a young 17-year-old from Germany looking for a home at the last minute because his placement in Arizona fell through. That's how we wound up with the student name Pascal. Little did I know that his coming to live with us would change the direction of my life forever!

An International Perspective

Little-known fact: ballroom dancing in Europe is the third most popular sport — in fact, it's common for little kids to learn it as they grow up. So, six months after Pascal got here, he wanted to check out the only dance studio in our town. My mom asked me to go along, since she would be unable to do so regularly and would need to have me drive him. Begrudgingly, I said yes.

Now, picture this: I was a football-looking kid. I was 6-foot-2, 240 pounds, and looked like a lineman. I wore baggy clothes, clunky shoes, and had no body image. So I took a seat by the window and tried to blend into the background...but then I noticed there were a lot of pretty girls in that class. That made it easier to take!

My first picture with Sally and her Junior team

Who, Me?

Then the unthinkable happened: five minutes after I got there, Sally came over and said, "I desperately need some guys for this group class. Come help me."

I said, "You've gotta be kidding. I've got two left feet."

"That's okay," she said. "Some of my usual guys couldn't make it. I just need you to stand in today."

From an Uneasy Start...

When I was introduced to my partner, Honey, I was so nervous! I remember thinking how pretty she was, and how way out of my league I was — I found out later she was already in college, so not only was she beautiful, but older than me. I'd never had many dates in high school, and yet here I was,

My first dance partner, Honey

INTRODUCTION / From an Uneasy Start

not only getting to be with a lovely girl, but holding her. It was a life-changing experience in more ways than one!

My first lesson was the most awkward, uncomfortable time I'd ever had…and yet, when the night was over, I was excited. I had just done something way more fun than anything else I'd ever done in my life. I liked it better than football, wrestling, baseball — all the different sports I played growing up — even though I was horrible at it. So I offered to drive each week, and slowly I got a little bit better and felt less clumsy. I was still really uncomfortable and nervous around Honey, but miracle of miracles, she didn't seem uncomfortable at all. She actually seemed to like dancing with me. So when, a few months later, Pascal decided to pursue other things and dropped dancing, I kept going. I even stepped in for Pascal at a competition. We did great at the show, and for the next few years, I had the time of my life.

INTRODUCTION / Higher Education

Higher Education

When I went to college, because I'd always had a knack for art and artistic things, I thought I'd do graphic design and video production. On the first day of class, as I was walking on campus, I looked down on the sidewalk and saw a piece of paper taped to the ground talking about the Purdue ballroom dance team. They were having a "callout," or meeting, to get acquainted with potential dancers. I went to the callout — along with 350 other people! After the ballroom team performed for all of us, they gave a first lesson. Naturally, I already knew the beginner steps — and all the girls wanted to dance with me because of it. Suddenly, I was Mr. Popular, a complete 180-degree turn from high school.

Ballroom was quickly becoming my driving passion. After graduating in 2008 I knew I wanted to move to Indianapolis, but with the downturn of the economy, graphic design jobs even there were scarce. When I told my dance partner about it, she said, "No problem." As it turned out, her parents were part of a ballroom dance studio in Carmel, Indiana (near Indianapolis), and she thought that I would be a great part of that studio. So, two weeks after graduation, I drove Indianapolis to find the studio in Carmel. Sure, I was nervous — but at that point, I had more confidence in ballroom than I did in graphic design!

After a quick conversation with the manager, in which he discovered I had seven years' experience, he asked me if I could start the following Monday. I was dumbfounded: back at Purdue, my friends were all struggling for jobs, but I'd just had the easiest job application process ever.

To my way of thinking, this was the best of both worlds. My hours at the studio allowed for regular job searches (for a real adult grownup job!), so I gave myself six months at the dance studio to do so. Only trouble was, I was having way too much fun at the studio! But, as things turned out, I got a roommate who was also a Purdue alum, and we went to a local church where we joined the young 20-somethings group. Through this group, I met my wife, and we were married in October 2010…when I was still part of the dance studio. Now, I'm sure you're thinking, "Wait a minute. That's more than six months!"

It sure is! At this point, I'd been dancing for eleven years and professionally teaching it for four. And, incidentally, through teaching dance I've learned everything I know about sales. The first thing I learned over time — and something that's still invaluable today — was the importance of that first impression.

It only took me 2 hours to realize I just got a sales position

The price of one 45 minute dance lesson with me was $145. And that was in 2008 just as the great recession hit. Probably not the best time to have landed what I thought was a dance instructor's job, but really turned out to be a sales job. You see, it was my job to find my students, sell them into taking lessons from me, and keep them for life.

Not an easy thing for a wet-behind-the-ears kid just out of college.

I started at the dance studio on a very low base salary with commissions after I hit a certain amount. But it wasn't long before I was strict commission. Whenever anyone cancelled, my pay for that 45 minutes went from something to nothing. If I couldn't find someone else to fill the spot, I was sitting around freely twiddling my thumbs.

INTRODUCTION / Higher Education

Fortunately for me, I had some wise parents who had taught me well about financial responsibility so my $2,000 college loan was paid off in 3 months after leaving college and with a paid off car and no credit card debt, my expenses were pretty minimal. I could weather the poverty income I made that first 9 months at the studio.

But little by little I learned how to sell from the owner of the studio. Yes, I had to develop my own style, but I am glad to have been mentored by this wise business owner.

And it paid off.

In the 4 years I was at the studio I sold over $700,000 in dance lessons and I had many students stay with me the entire 4 years I was there.

As much for myself as for others who might read this book, I decided to write it all down.

While I no longer teach dance, the lessons I took with me still apply in my new career as an actual sales executive. The ballroom dance floor might seem to be a strange place to learn sales, but in my case I'm forever thankful for the experience.

Tyler Hershberger
317-620-1212

INTRODUCTION / Higher Education

My first competitive partner, Jasmine. Still in high school

Jasmin and me in competition at Notre Dame

Jasmin and me accepting our first place ribbon

Notice all the metals Jasmin and I won

Our men's ballroom showcase routine

EVERYTHING I LEARNED ABOUT SALES AND SUCCESS
I LEARNED ON THE BALLROOM DANCE FLOOR

INTRODUCTION / Higher Education

Competing on the Purdue Ballroom Team

My sister, Anya and me dancing during college

Dancing with one of my students during my professional days

Chapter 1

That First 4 Seconds

As I learned how to dance, I also learned what made people comfortable or uncomfortable; how I could connect with women and relax their male partners at the same time. I learned how to get a feel for people, and I realized they were checking me out as well. Was I polite? Warm? Friendly? Standoffish? Did I have any personal quirks that they didn't like? It all counts, from your appearance to the way you introduce yourself and speak to people.

And make no mistake — in this, as in many other aspects, men and women are different. In those first four seconds, a man will automatically size another guy up; for guys, it's all about respect. Does he look clean, and not over the top? Does he seem intelligent but not cocky? And, most importantly, can I trust him?

Whatever you're doing in life, you need to make a good impression. And never assume people don't notice; they do. Many first impressions are made without knowing it. One time after coming back from dinner, I realized that my new students, unknown to me at the moment, had been sitting next to us in the restaurant. They'd had a good chance to see me make a first impression…when I hadn't even known I was doing it. Remember: those first four seconds can mean everything!

Chapter 2

Cut the Drama — Just Dance

I went through a lot of nerves when I first tried to dance. I was all caught up in how beautiful Honey was, and how I'd never been very popular with girls in school; if I'd have let that drama control my actions, I'd never have discovered my calling. Same goes with too much drama in your life, either professionally or personally. We all know people who seem to thrive on drama, but the truth is that very rarely is drama happy or uplifting to most of us. Some folks enjoy watching it; otherwise, reality shows wouldn't be so popular! But most people hate being caught in the middle, and for good reason: drama can ruin the energy in any environment.

CHAPTER 2 / Cut the Drama — Just Dance

I like to compare drama to a tornado. If you're far enough away, you can't take your eyes off it. If you live in the same state, you hear about it or see it on TV. If you are close, you get sucked in—even if you don't want to be. It rips apart and mangles everything it touches. And in the end, whatever or whoever caused it are not the ones who have to clean up the wreckage.

People feed off energy. So if your energy is dark and drama-filled, you will repel people like a magnet. Most people have an instinct about these things, and they'll avoid that energy black hole. If you are relaxed and happy, on the other hand, then people will enjoy being around you.

Chapter 3

Dance like No One's Looking

At least one popular song over the years has had lyrics about dancing "like no one's looking." The idea seems to be that if you forget about whether anyone's watching you or not, you'll be able to loosen up and let your true talent/spirit/enthusiasm out. Sounds good, doesn't it? I don't like this saying, though. To me, it basically conveys the opposite idea of loosening up; it conveys the idea that, in fact, people are always watching you…you're just supposed to pretend that they're not. Now, that's relaxing, isn't it? NOT.

Let's face it: if you dance as if you're always being watched, then you will never be comfortable or enjoy yourself. The same concept applies to sales. Never expect to be great—or even that good—at something new. Even if you are just changing to a different type of sales, you should expect to have a learning curve. Everywhere you go, pressure is being applied to you, so don't add your own on top of it. Give yourself time to learn and relax. I give the same advice to every student I teach, especially the men. They tend to overcomplicate things and get frustrated —until they stop trying to master everything and just have fun.

Chapter 4

A $140,000 Sale in 15 Minutes

Have you ever made a really, really fast sale? This was one of mine…sort of. Actually, the $140,000 was spread over time. But it happened through the power of something we all know about in sales but often don't do: maximize the referral.

It's a simple tool to use, really. If your customers are happy, chances are they're talking about you to somebody. What you want to know is who those somebodies are! How do you learn these names? ASK. That's how I got a $140,000 sale in 15 minutes: I asked a student if she knew anyone else that wanted to dance. With the immense popularity of dancing shows, more often than not, that answer's going to be YES. Then, you take that "yes" and that referral…and fly with it. Technically, it's not making money without working for it at all…but it can often be the next best thing!

Chapter 5

The Most Important Word in Selling Has Only Three Letters

Can you guess what they are?

No, those letters aren't Y-O-U. They're not even Y-E-S — although that's what we're all bouncing out of bed every morning trying to get to, aren't we? We want to find the "yeses" among all the "nos" or "not-sures" or "maybe-laters".

So what are those three important letters? F-U-N!

If you like to have fun, you're automatically attractive to people. People who are having FUN doing what they do bring others on board almost effortlessly. Fun is contagious. Fun is enticing. Fun is what all of us need more of. We know it. You know it. So if people see you having FUN doing what you're doing — the sale has already happened. Just have the FUN of reeling it in and prospering!

Chapter 6

How I Found Hidden Objections

While dancing with my students, my goal was to get them laughing and talking. I knew that if they were talking about what was going on in their lives, they would help me help them in two different ways. First, they'd reveal what may be hidden objections to a sale; second, they'd usually also give me insights into what would make them stay.

When you get people relaxed and talking in an enjoyable environment, you'll find out tons more information than you'll get by trying to control the situation with questions you've planned out ahead of time. By all means ask questions to get people to open up. But then, be quiet and let them. The best salespeople are all really, really good listeners. You want to be one of them!

Chapter 7

The Art of the Dance Is Magic in Selling

Sales and dance have a crucial ingredient in common: trust. The best dance teams dance as one, but that's because each partner trusts the other implicitly to do what they've rehearsed, the way they rehearsed it. If you don't trust your partner, you will never move through the awkward learning stage to the enjoyment side of dance. But once you've got that solid trust in your partner, you don't try to do too much on your own. No soloist can win a couples' dance competition!

Likewise, no salesperson sells all by him or herself. The prospect has to cooperate. In order to get that cooperation, however, you need to build trust first. If, for whatever reason a person doesn't trust you, no matter how badly they need what you have, they won't believe you have their best interests at heart, and they'll walk away.

Dancing is an art. You get to experience music, movement, and emotions without ever uttering a word. Selling is the same.

Chapter 8

Automate to Organize

When you get to a high level of expertise in anything, you say it's automatic. Sometimes, that's a figure of speech…but sometimes, it's priceless to be able to literally have things automatic. Standard procedures don't have to stifle creativity. In most instances, they enhance it — they free the artist to concentrate on what he or she does best instead of being awash in administrative or other details.

The same goes for a dance studio. In order to teach an effective lesson, our studio used a standard curriculum. This helped me stay on task each lesson, ultimately allowing me to bring more of my personality into my teaching style. Standard operating procedure, when it's efficient and consistent, leads to great creative results.

CHAPTER 9 / Dancing Is All about Confidence

Chapter 9

Dancing Is All about Confidence

Let's face it, guys: when we're learning anything new, we tend to be shaky. We all have a fear of looking bad in front of others. If we're at home with no one watching us, we're more willing and able to go out on a limb — but get strangers' eyes on us and we freeze up.

Want to see this in action? Go to any bar or club in America and look at the dance floor. You'll see some couples dancing, maybe a co-ed group or two, but most of them will be groups of girls. Where are the guys? Mostly sitting at the tables. Why? Do they not like girls? Do they not like music? Neither is true. The fact is, most of them don't feel comfortable dancing. Most of us don't learn how to dance as a routine part of growing up — so guys are especially apprehensive about it.

Believe me, dancing is a learned skill. Some might have more of a natural knack for it, but anyone can learn. So in the end, it all boils down to confidence. The only way to gain confidence is to slowly build it up. If those guys would go out for one song one week, then two the next, then three the week after that, soon they would be out there all the time. But that initial fear is hard to get past. The same goes for selling. Some folks are naturals at it, but even they need to learn and keep learning to improve. And the rest of us might start out shaky…but as we practice, we'll gain confidence.

# Chapter 10

How to Look Your Best: the Sale before the Sale

Appearances matter. We all know it. But being comfortable in your own skin is important, too. How to strike a great balance? Know whom you're about to talk to.

Looking your best means different things in different circumstances. For example, if you're going into a very casual situation, with a person who's very laid-back, being spit-and-polish in suit and tie might be professional, but it might also be intimidating. It can make your client feel uneasy about how approachable you are, how down-to-earth, or how like them you might be. And all those things can get in the way of the rapport and trust you want with the people you meet.

Remember: your ultimate goal is to help whomever you're talking to relax. A lot of that comes from how you present yourself and how you feel. If you look great but don't feel great, the person you're talking to will pick up on that…and you don't want either of you to be uncomfortable. Know as much as possible about the person you're meeting beforehand, but don't underestimate the value of your own instincts, too. If you're relaxed and friendly, it goes a long way toward making the most of any conversation you have.

Chapter 11

How I Learned to Remember Names and Faces

Are you good with names? Faces? Some folks are. Me…I have struggled with this my whole life. In college, as a joke, I bought a shirt that had written on the front, "What's your name again?" Fact is it helped me out of more than one jam!

Once I became a teacher, I knew I probably couldn't rely on a cute T-shirt slogan to get by. And I knew that if I kept forgetting my students' names, I would find myself without students very quickly. The method that worked for me the best in this situation? A picture was worth a thousand words. After a few lessons, I took a photo with them and put it in their syllabus. Then, as I planned their lesson, I would look at their pictures and read their names.

Now, I still struggle with names once in a while… but I never forget a face. And that's half the battle already won!

Chapter 12

How I Find New Customers and Keep Old Ones

Keeping customers is easy: just pay attention to them when paying attention to them isn't easy!

Sound like double-talk? It's not, really. Just think about it. It's easy to talk to your customers when they're right in front of you. Then, it's easy to lavish attention on them. But how about when they're not around? How about sending them a handwritten card on their birthdays? How about calling a customer to find out how his/her son did in baseball the night before, or how their daughter is doing in her musical pursuits? Ever think to send flowers to a customer when they're in the hospital?

You might not have thought of these things, but you'll want to think of them in the future. I've discovered that if I forget to keep up with my customers, they forget to keep coming to their lessons. When I remember to do the little things like this, however, they not only keep coming back, but they send their friends and neighbors in, too. In today's world, a little kindness isn't a little thing. It's not only a wonderful way to reach out to people, but it's your best walking advertisement…day in and day out. Keep it in mind!

Chapter 13

"Two Left Feet"? No Problem!

If I've heard this one once, I've heard it a thousand times. I even used it myself, once upon a time (remember my early story?). "Dance lessons would be a waste for me. I've got two left feet." The "two left feet" objection covers a lot of territory, even outside dance lessons. So how to counter it?

The best way I heard this handled was, "Great! We have a bunch of rights in the back. I'll trade ya." Once people laugh at that, you've just defused that objection. They relax; they know their excuse is forgiven — without losing face. And in reality, people make this objection most often simply because they're shy…or scared. Help them out.

Take the pressure out of the situation; in effect, convey to them that it's okay (and understandable) to be scared, but it doesn't have to hold them back. Soon, they'll see that for themselves. And then, they become some of your most fearless supporters.

Chapter 14

Enthusiasm-Boosters

Enthusiasm, like any other attitude, is contagious — with the added plus that it makes whatever you're doing much easier. When you're having fun, your customers will catch enthusiasm from you, relax, and enjoy themselves. It's only natural. Do everything possible to make your customers' experience so good they can't wait for the next lesson. When you see their eyes light up, you know you're doing it right…and you're going to keep them coming back for more of that great feeling!

Chapter 15

An Amazing Closing Technique I Learned from a 35-year-old Dance Veteran

The best sales people know not to try too hard. In other words…they don't push. They don't press. And they don't try to force any sale to close before its time.

How do you do this? Take a few steps backward emotionally and allow prospects to close themselves. It's amazing how often this happens, if you're only willing (and brave enough!) to let the game come to you. If you have presented the options in an easy, simple way, then all you need to do is enjoy the conversation. The more fun and relaxed you are, the less pressure they will feel. Bottom line is: just shut up!

Chapter 16

Don't Be Afraid to Fail

Dancing isn't for everybody. You might love it so much you think everyone should do it — and I hope you do love it that much, if you're teaching it and selling lessons! But not everyone's going to fall in love with it. By no means did everyone I ever introduce to dancing love it as much as I did. If I'd worried too much about that, I would have thought I'd failed. But in reality…I hadn't.

The plain fact is, some folks will always say no. They just won't bite. Don't take it personally; they're not saying you're off base for loving what you do enough that you want everyone to have the pleasure of the experience. They're simply saying it's not for them. As long as you remember that, and don't despair over those few, you'll stay positive. And that positive, upbeat attitude will magnetically draw the right ones to you.

Everyone's Got Rhythm

Do you have rhythm? You might be surprised by the answer!

Human beings, like every other created thing in the universe, have a natural rhythm. We don't all have the same rhythm or pace —we don't all march to the same drummer. But we all have an internal beat, even if we're unaware of it. So when people say to you, "I don't have rhythm," they're in for a fun surprise.

I actually loved this excuse, because it was the easiest one to overcome. I just asked them to walk across the floor, and then pointed out that they walked with a steady rhythm. Once people realize that the simple act of walking proves rhythm's not a mysterious talent for only a few, they're tickled. And when people are tickled by something they can do, they don't feel sold or manipulated into taking the next step. Remember: it's a natural step…something they've already got. The next steps to building on that talent can then come just as naturally.

Chapter 22

If all else fails, remember:

- Just keep counting to eight
- Keep with the beat
- Break dancing, dirty dancing, square dancing, and other marketplace oddities — get creative with your approaches
- Ginger Rogers did everything Fred Astaire did — backwards and in heels
- "Dancing with the Stars" proves it still pays to do all the work and get half the glory
- People hate to be sold…but they want to buy
- Make it look easy and smile like you're having fun…no matter what
- Automate the follow-up
- Just keep counting to eight

Epilog

When I got married in 2010 I knew my ballroom dance instructing days were numbered. While I was having a blast, I also wanted to be with my wife - and nights and weekend hours (she worked days) didn't allow that to happen.

So I had to begin looking for a new job.

99% of people look for a job by going to online job posting websites. My mother always told me the best jobs are not being advertised. The secret is to find a golden needle in a very large haystack. Not an easy task, but well worth the final results.

I did a really risky thing, though. I quit my job before I found that golden needle (i.e. had a new job). But it did allow me to focus 100% on my job hunting efforts. Those sales lessons on the ballroom floor were about to tested.

My Job Hunting Strategy

I decided to hire my local postman to help me hunt for a job. For the price of a stamp, he would deliver anything I wanted him to, to the very person I wanted it to go to.

He could open the doors and I could do what I do best – close the deal.

I live in Indianapolis, Indiana. In Indiana there is a list of the top 100 companies to work for in the state. Of those 100, 38 were in Indianapolis. Since I had a degree in video production from Purdue I also researched and found the addresses for all the video production companies in the Indianapolis area.

My entire mailing list ended up being 48 companies.

They were my "haystack".

I grew up with a mother who LOVES marketing and has written a number of million dollar direct mail campaigns for clients. I figured it might be a good idea to see if she'd help me out.

Life was good when after beginning my 5-step

EPILOG

direct mail campaign to those 48 companies, my phone began to ring every day with interviews and finally job offers.

My golden needle ended up being 12 Stars Media – a very creative video production company with clients like Thermo Scientific, Indianapolis Children's Museum, MaxIT Healthcare, Indiana University Health, and Simon Malls. I became their Account Manager.

I will always be grateful for my time in the ballroom dance world. Whether it's dancing a Cha Cha, Waltz, Foxtrot, Rumba, Swing, Hustle, or Tango it will always be part of me. It was on the ballroom dance floor I found my passion for sales.

Rocky Walls, CEO of 12 Stars Media with me

www.ingramcontent.com/pod-product-compliance
Lightning Source LLC
Chambersburg PA
CBHW071649170526
45166CB00003B/1491